HAL•LEONARD
INSTRUMENTAL
PLAY-ALONG

AUDIO ACCESS
INCLUDED

FLUTE

Piazzolla Tangos

To access audio visit:
www.halleonard.com/mylibrary

3054-5997-7375-9913

ISBN 978-1-4950-2839-7

BOOSEY & HAWKES

AN IMAGEM COMPANY

DISTRIBUTED BY

HAL•LEONARD®
CORPORATION
7777 W. BLUEMOUND RD. P.O. BOX 13819 MILWAUKEE, WI 53213

www.boosey.com
www.halleonard.com

AUSENCIAS
(The Absent)

FLUTE

ASTOR PIAZZOLLA

EL VIAJE
(The Voyage)

FLUTE

ASTOR PIAZZOLLA

CHANSON DE LA NAISSANCE
(Song of the Birth)
from FAMILLE D'ARTISTES

FLUTE

ASTOR PIAZZOLLA

MILONGA
from A MIDSUMMER NIGHT'S DREAM

FLUTE

ASTOR PIAZZOLLA

LIBERTANGO

FLUTE

ASTOR PIAZZOLLA

LOS SUEÑOS
(Dreams)
from SUR

FLUTE

ASTOR PIAZZOLLA

OBLIVION

FLUTE

ASTOR PIAZZOLLA

OUVERTURE
from FAMILLE D'ARTISTES

FLUTE

ASTOR PIAZZOLLA

SENSUEL
(Sensual)
from A MIDSUMMER NIGHT'S DREAM

FLUTE

ASTOR PIAZZOLLA

SENTIMENTAL
from FAMILLE D'ARTISTES

FLUTE

ASTOR PIAZZOLLA

VUELVO AL SUR
(I'm Returning South)

FLUTE

ASTOR PIAZZOLLA

SIN RUMBO
(Aimless)

FLUTE

ASTOR PIAZZOLLA

STREET TANGO

FLUTE

ASTOR PIAZZOLLA

TANGO FINAL
from FAMILLE D'ARTISTES

FLUTE

ASTOR PIAZZOLLA

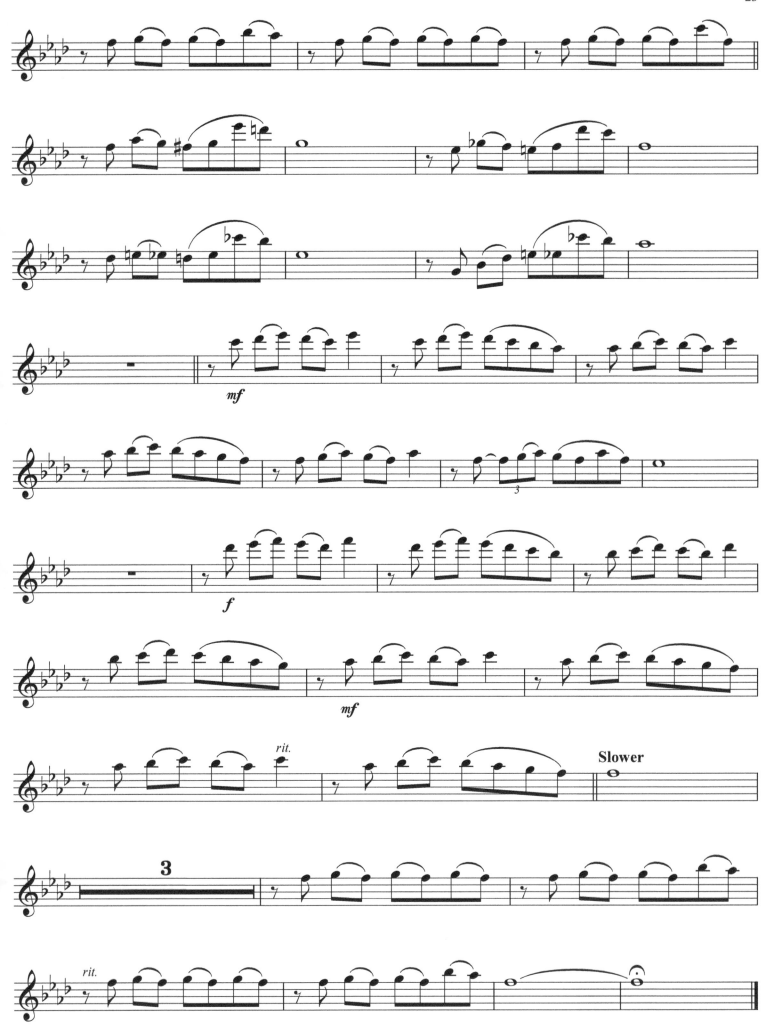